Bertolt Brecht

by MARTIN ESSLIN

Columbia University Press

NEW YORK & LONDON 1969

COLUMBIA ESSAYS ON MODERN WRITERS is a series of critical studies of English, Continental, and other writers whose works are of contemporary artistic and intellectual significance.

Editor: William York Tindall

Advisory Editors

Jacques Barzun   W. T. H. Jackson   Joseph A. Mazzeo

Bertolt Brecht is Number 42 of the series

MARTIN ESSLIN is Head of Drama (Radio) at the B.B.C. He is the author of *Brecht: The Man and His Work* and *The Theatre of the Absurd.*

Acknowledgment is made to Methuen & Company, Ltd., for permission to quote from Bertolt Brecht's *Tales from the Calendar,* translated by Yvonne Kapp and Michael Hamburger.

Bertolt Brecht

In the edition of Bertolt Brecht's works which his West German publishers issued to commemorate the seventieth anniversary of his birth (1968)—and which, for all its omissions and editorial imperfections, is likely to remain the fullest and most nearly complete corpus of Brecht's *œuvre* for a very long time to come —just over three thousand pages are occupied by his dramatic output; over a thousand by his poetry; fifteen hundred by his novels and stories; and well over two thousand by his theoretical essays on aesthetics and politics. It is an impressive body of work; and one must always keep in mind that a very large proportion of it remains untranslated into English; the fact that the bulk of the translations are of plays and that only relatively few poems, essays, and stories are accessible to the English-speaking public has a distorting effect on Brecht's image in the English-speaking world. It may indeed sound heretical today, but may well be true nevertheless, that posterity might attribute greater importance to Brecht's poems and some of his short stories than to his work as a dramatist; or that of his twenty-one full-length and sixteen shorter plays, and six major adaptations, perhaps no more than half a dozen might stand the test of time. As to his theoretical writings, they have played an important part in creating Brecht's world-wide fame, for they have stimulated discussion about his plays among actors, directors, and critics and have made the study of his work particularly attractive in academic circles. They might, however, also prove the most vulnerable element in Brecht's posthumous reputation, resting, as they do, on the fairly shaky foundations of Brecht's own peculiar view of Marxism, a very questionable conception of the psychological basis of the audience's experience in the theatre, and on many passing fashions of the political and aesthetic climate of his times.

Much of Brecht's future reputation will also depend on another vital element in his artistic personality: his work as a practical man of the theatre, as a teacher of actors and directors. Brecht's sudden rise to world fame in the last years of his life was, in fact, primarily due to the success of his theatre, the Berliner Ensemble, which he founded, after his return from exile, in 1949, and which took Paris by storm on the occasion of the international festival of 1954. The Berliner Ensemble was created to test Brecht's theory of drama in performance; in the second decade after Brecht's death it still keeps its reputation as one of the world's foremost companies; but hitherto it has failed to produce any dramatist of note who could be said to have developed his own style on the basis of Brecht's theories; and the danger that it might decline into a mere museum of Brecht's own productions is therefore certainly not yet banished.

In the English-speaking world and in France Brecht's reputation has, as it were, been standing on its head: his work as a director (largely in the spheres unaffected by ignorance of the text—design, lighting, music) came first and has exercised the deepest influence; then, because it stimulated fruitful and endlessly interesting discussion, came his work as a theorist of left-wing aesthetics; and only in the third place there followed his output as a dramatist, with far less convincing success. Whether in France, Britain, or America, relatively few of Brecht's plays have really achieved a decisive breakthrough and many have

[4]

been signal failures. And Brecht the great poet and prose writer is virtually unknown.

Yet it is this aspect of Brecht that should come first. That many of his plays remain failures in translation is often directly attributable to the fact that in German they succeed mainly by the force of their language, their poetry, far less so as drama.

No wonder, therefore, that meaningful discussion of Brecht is very difficult in English, that a great deal of the vast literature which has grown around him and continues to proliferate has an air of irreality and is bedeviled by fierce controversy directly attributable to the widely differing basic assumptions from which different commentators derive the starting point for their arguments. And this situation, already complex enough, is further complicated by the highly inflammable political content of Brecht's work.

Brecht was converted to Communism before he was thirty and remained a Communist to the end of his life; yet much depends on the *nature* of his Communism: it would be equally naïve to regard Brecht as a mere follower of the party line at any given period or to label him a consistent deviationist; to assume that his ostensible support of, say, the Stalinist show trials also implied support for Stalinist aesthetics—or, conversely, that having been accused of being a formalist by the supporters of orthodox Stalinist aesthetics, he must also have disapproved of Stalinist policies in other fields.

What all this ultimately amounts to is the need to reiterate again and again the obvious, yet frequently ignored, truism that to understand Brecht one must see him against his background: the background of his language and its culture and literature, the background of the history of his times, the background of the theatre against which he rebelled, the background of Marxist theory and Marxist politics.

Brecht was born at Augsburg, the chief town of the Bavarian

part of Swabia, on February 10, 1898; he thus belongs to the generation who reached their maturity in World War I. When the war ended in 1918 Brecht was almost twenty-one and ready to take the plunge into the whirlpool of experimentation—in life as well as in art—which was the inevitable consequence of the collapse of the hallowed—now seen to be hollow—values of respectable Wilhelminian society that, only a few years earlier, had seemed immovable and eternally stable. The feeling of liberation which the breakup and sudden disappearance of that social order produced was exhilarating, but at the same time it must also have been very frightening to be propelled directly from the strait jacket of small-town petty bourgeois gentility into the void of almost total permissiveness. Brecht's later decision to subject himself to the new strait jacket of party discipline—and, indeed, the whole German nation's equally morbid drive to do likewise in the acceptance of the iron rule of Hitler—must be seen in the light of this experience.

The first phase of Brecht's career as a writer represents the period of that liberation into nothingness (*ca.* 1918–*ca.* 1927); it produced the plays *Baal, Drums in the Night, In the Jungle of the Cities, Edward II, A Man's a Man,* and culminated in the *Threepenny Opera* and *Mahagonny* (the last two written after 1927 but still imbued with an afterglow of that period) and the volume of poems *Hauspostille.* This phase of anarchic nihilism was followed by a period of austere didacticism, a frantic search for discipline (*ca.* 1927–*ca.* 1934) which resulted in the most severely controlled, the seemingly—but only seemingly—most arid portion of Brecht's *œuvre,* the *Lehrstücke* and *Schulopern* (teaching plays and school operas) *The Didactic Play of Baden on Consent, The Flight of the Lindberghs, He Who Says Yes/ He Who Says No, The Measures Taken, The Exception and the Rule,* and *The Horatians and the Curiatians,* as well as the more "conventional" but nonetheless highly austere political plays *St. Joan of the Stockyards*, *The Mother* (after Gorky), and *The Roundheads and the Peakheads*. The volume of poems which represents this phase is *Lieder, Gedichte, Chöre*, a compendium of strictly propagandist poems and songs which forms a complete contrast to the wild exuberance and parodistic anarchism of *Hauspostille*.

In the first years of exile, particularly in the period of the Popular Front, when the Communist party sought the cooperation of all liberal and left-wing forces against the Nazi danger, the uncompromising all-or-nothing attitude of this didactic phase was clearly out of place, and gave way to a brief period (1934–38) of openly propagandistic writing in more conventional styles. The *Threepenny Novel* and the plays *Fears and Miseries of the Third Reich* and *Señora Carrar's Rifles* were the products of this period in Brecht's life as a writer.

After the threat of world war became only too obvious following the Nazi occupation of Vienna and the Munich crisis (1938), the chances of influencing the course of events by writing propaganda were clearly reduced to zero; this freed Brecht and enabled him to turn his creative energies back to more personal poetry and the composition of his most mature and greatest series of plays. In this period (*ca.* 1938–*ca.* 1947) he wrote *Mother Courage, The Good Woman of Setzuan, Arturo Ui, Puntila, The Life of Galileo, The Visions of Simone Machard*, and *The Caucasian Chalk Circle* as well as some of his most deeply felt poetry (contained, together with some propaganda verse from the preceding phase, in the volume *Svendborger Gedichte*).

Following his return to Europe from the United States (where he lived from the summer of 1941 to the fall of 1947), Brecht concentrated on his theoretical writings and his work as

[7]

artistic director of his own theatre. His output as a playwright in this period (1947 to his death in 1956) is disappointing both in quantity and in quality. Apart from minor original plays (*The Days of the Commune, Turandot or the Congress of White-washers*) his work for the theatre consists largely of adaptations: *Antigone* (after Sophocles in Hölderlin's German version), *The Tutor* (after Reinhold Michael Lenz), *Don Juan* (after Molière), *The Trial of Joan of Arc at Rouen* (after a radio play by Anna Seghers based on the record of Joan's actual trial), *Trumpets and Drums* (after Farquhar's *The Recruiting Officer*), and *Coriolanus.* On the other hand, in this phase of relatively low creativity as a playwright, Brecht found an outlet for his emotions (of resignation at the coming of old age, of disillusionment with the philistine East German regime) in what must be regarded as his finest achievement as a lyrical poet: a body of elegantly elegiac, sadly ironical, highly economical free verse.

Brecht's career thus shows a clear pattern of development and its own dialectic: anarchic exuberance (1918–*ca.* 1927) abruptly turning to the opposite extreme, austere self-discipline (*ca.* 1927–1934); a brief interlude of openly propagandist, almost journalistic, work, undertaken to help the good cause of anti-Fascism (1934–38); then, as a synthesis of emotional exuberance, severe Marxist rationalism, and some elements of political special pleading, the great works of the mature phase (1938–47); and, finally, to crown the whole, the period from Brecht's return to Europe to his death (1947–56) when in the theatre he fulfilled his theories by his practice as a great director, while, as a lyrical poet, he reached sublime heights of detached self-knowledge and melancholic self-irony. It is a pattern which bears the marks of the great career of a great man.

The anarchic exuberance of the youth and the severe rationalism of the Marxist find their common denominator, however, in the concept of rebellion: the adolescent rebelled against the narrowness of small-town life, of desiccated stiff-collared bourgeois teachers, the musty smell of respectability and sexual repression; the Marxist clung to self-discipline and Spartan abnegation of self (including its anarchic longings for freedom) only in order to accomplish effective rebellion against the social order which had produced two wars and National Socialism. The recognition that rebellion to accomplish freedom can only succeed if the rebel's own freedom is ruthlessly suppressed in the discipline of party forms the ironical, yet tragic, *leitmotiv* of Brecht's *œuvre*. This ambivalence—which must also be seen as a highly characteristic German quality—explains the fascination which the Hegelian dialectic held for Brecht; it is also the basis of his genius as a dramatist.

For what is a playwright if he is not an individual who can experience and express a multitude of contradictory impulses and passions with equal comprehension and empathy for *each* of them? Just as Shakespeare could momentarily assume the personality of Iago as well as Othello, of Shylock as well as Antonio, Brecht also was able to be at the same time Garga and Shlink, Joan Dark and Mauler, Galilei and the Grand Inquisitor, Edward II and Mortimer, MacHeath and Peachum, dumb Katrin and Mother Courage. But he went further: the tensions and contradictions often actually split Brecht's characters wide open. Anna I and Anna II in the ballet *The Seven Deadly Sins* express the emotional and rational components of the *same* girl and are the forerunners of a line of dialectical characters: Shen Te/Shui Ta in *The Good Woman of Setzuan;* Puntila, who is good when drunk and evil when sober; Azdak, who can be a good Judge only because he is a rascal; Mother Courage, who is destructive in her professional capacity as a businesswoman profiting from war and a positive character in being a mother intent on keeping her children alive and well; Galilei, whose

[9]

sensuality and cowardice are balanced by his heroic greatness as a scientist. At the base of this deeply ambivalent attitude toward the world there is a sense of deep disillusionment. World War I was the end not only of an epoch but of a whole system of values in Germany. And Brecht belonged to the generation which had to grow up into this moon landscape of collapse and bankruptcy. Brecht's early poetry is full of images of despair. "The blind," he says in one passage, "talk about a way out. But *I* can see." And elsewhere he speaks about an epoch when the tables of the law itself have crumbled and not even sleeping with one's own sister gives pleasure any more. There is a persistent feeling of guilt in these early poems, disgust with sex and life, and a wild strain of accusation against God, who, it is said, does not exist, but "how can *that* not exist, which can betray man so deeply?" Thus the existence of God, an evil, malevolent force, is postulated to explain the measure of·suffering and corruption in the world. As to the Devil—he too has become inefficient and lazy. It is no longer worth while to lie; from sheer despair men speak the truth, unaware of the danger of speaking the truth. "And the Devil no longer takes his best customers."

Passages like these, which Brecht wrote in his early twenties, for all their adolescent pose of cynical world-weariness, show the background of horror which must always be kept in mind in trying to understand Brecht's later political commitment. Only the experience of the desolation caused by so total a collapse of values can explain the frantic search for a new set of values to replace those which have been discredited, only the emptiness of total isolation in a world deprived of all social ties can account for the frantic craving for a new collective consciousness, for the discipline and fellow-feeling engendered by merging into a dedicated fellowship of fighters like the Communist party. When even murder had become too strenuous

[10]

for the disillusioned, then even the will to violence could appear as a positive value:

> Terrible is it to kill.
> But not only others, ourselves too, we must kill, if necessary
> For this world, this killing world, can only
> Be changed by violence, as
> All living beings know.
> As yet, we said, it is not granted to us
> To be able not to kill. Only with our
> Unbending will to alter the world we justified
> The measure we took.

Thus do the four agitators (i.e., party activists) in Brecht's starkest tragedy, *Die Massnahme* (The Measures Taken, 1930), justify the liquidation of their young comrade who had broken the iron rules of discipline. It is the horror of the world which justifies the horror of the measures which have to be taken to alter the world. If man's meanness to his fellow-men, his greed and brutality are merely the product of irrational and fossilized property relations, then a rational organization of society *would* enable the inherent goodness of man's nature to assert itself; greed and selfishness, meanness and brutality would disappear from the earth. This essentially Rousseauist rejection of the concept of original sin (which is indeed one of the basic assumptions of Marxism) plays an immense part in Brecht's political and also in his aesthetic thought. For Brecht's theory of drama—the *epic* or, later, the *dialectical* theatre with its *Verfremdungseffekt* (wrongly translated as "Alienation" effect, more correctly as "strange-making effect")—ultimately stems from his conviction that Aristotle's definition of the *dramatic* as distinct from the *epic* form of poetry implied the notion of an unchanging and *unchangeable* human nature.

In their famous essay *On Epic and Dramatic Poetry* (1797) Goethe and Schiller asserted that the "great, essential difference" between the two kinds of literature "lies in the fact that

[11]

the epic poet presents the event as totally past, while the dramatic poet presents it as totally present." If the foundation of Marxism, Brecht argued, is the notion that the world can only be apprehended rationally as a dialectical, historical *process*, in the course of which all human values are in constant flux, ever changing, then this conception of drama was not only un-Marxist but, if accepted, a complete denial of everything that Marxism stood for. After all, if audiences could not only be brought face to face with the world of Shakespeare, or Sophocles, or Goethe but could be made to experience the events in these plays as *totally present*, if they could suffer with Oedipus, rage with Othello, weep with Iphigenia, then the eternally unchanging sameness of human nature would be a proven fact and Marxism would have been refuted! Had not Goethe and Schiller expressly stated in their essay that the actor, in their definition of drama, "wants the spectators to participate exclusively in his actions and in his immediate surroundings so that they should feel the sufferings of his soul and body with him, share his embarrassments and forget their own personalities for the sake of his. . . . The listener and spectator . . . must not be allowed to rise to thoughtful contemplation; he must passionately follow the action; his imagination is completely silenced and must not be taxed; and even things that are being narrated must, as it were, be brought before the audience's eyes by the actor." If a contemporary spectator could be made to identify himself with Oedipus or Othello to the point of actually forgetting his own personality and *becoming* Oedipus and Othello, how could he ever, argued Brecht, be brought to realize that Othello and Oedipus had been men determined by the social systems of their times and therefore by definition inaccessible to any such identification on the part of twentieth-century man, determined as he is by totally different social and economic conditions?

[12]

There can be little doubt that Brecht's entire theory of a truly Marxist theatre springs from his angry reaction against the very essay by Goethe and Schiller we have just quoted. In Brecht's theatre the action must *not* take place in a total present, but in a strictly defined historical past—hence the streamers with precise dates for each scene in plays like *Mother Courage*; in Brecht's theatre the spectators must *not* be allowed to identify with the actors on stage to the extent of forgetting their own personalities—hence Brecht's striving for a multitude of *Verfremdungseffekte*, i.e., devices which would prevent identification to the point of annihilating the suspension of disbelief (e.g., the actors stepping out of their parts, or grotesque masks that clearly reveal them to be puppets, etc.). And, finally, the spectator in Brecht's theatre *must be made* to rise to thoughtful contemplation, must be led to detached critical reflection on the play and its meaning. For only a detached spectator could appreciate the *distance* between the historical characters, determined by the social relations of their time on the one hand and contemporary man on the other. Even the familiar, argued Brecht, would yield its message only when seen with new eyes, as though it were something never noticed before. It was because Newton was capable of perceiving a falling apple as a strange and wonderful phenomenon that he had discovered the laws of gravitation. Hence Brecht asked his audience, at the end of *The Exception and the Rule:*

> You have seen the familiar, which always happens.
> But we beg you:
> What is not strange, find it disquieting!
> What is ordinary, find it inexplicable!
> What is usual, let it astonish you!
> What seems the rule, recognize it as an abuse.
> And where you have recognized abuse,
> Put things right!

Brecht's theory of "epic—i.e., nondramatic—drama" can thus

be seen both as an earnest endeavor to find a *Marxist* aesthetic of the theatre and as an angry rejection of the official, classical aesthetic codified by those twin deities of the German cultural establishment, Goethe and Schiller.

The rise of German nationhood, belatedly achieved in 1871, was intimately linked with the search for a *national literature* (as, indeed, the search for the great American novel sprang from the need to reassert American nationhood and the emancipation of American letters from being a mere provincial variant of British culture!). To buttress the German claim to be a great nation rather than a motley collection of barbarous tribes (whose rulers refused to use the rude vernacular and insisted on speaking French right into the middle of the eighteenth century) the need was urgent for writers of unquestioned international stature, men who could equal a Dante, a Shakespeare, a Racine, a Calderon. The two demigods of Weimar triumphantly met that need; they dominated German nineteenth-century drama by engendering a large number of feeble and insipid imitators of their style. When Germany finally achieved the status of a great power under Prussian leadership, the "classics," their immediate predecessors, and their progeny were made the pivot of the new establishment's ideal of education and became the pinnacle of *Bildung;* indeed the ability to quote Goethe's *Faust* and Schiller's *Wallenstein* was—and still is—the badge of social status in German culture.

As a result the curriculum of schools and universities effectively distorted the true situation. By the very nature of their objective "the classics" were literary, academic, and highly respectable. Because they had been rude, uncouth, and irregular, on the other hand, the very considerable poets and dramatists of the Baroque period, for example, were almost totally neglected; the immense achievement of genuine folk drama, particularly in Austria and Bavaria (a brilliant South German

[14]

version of the *commedia dell' arte;* great writers like Nestroy or Raimund), was almost entirely ignored; and a number of dramatists who did not fit the pattern created by the classics were disregarded as freaks and eccentrics (great figures of the *Sturm und Drang* period like Reinhold Michael Lenz; drunken geniuses like Grabbe; revolutionaries like Georg Büchner).

It is against this background that Brecht's revolt must be seen. To him the ugliness and stupidity, the complacency and smugness of the German *bourgeoisie* were personified by the pompous teachers at his *Gymnasium,* by the tired, routine performances of the "classics" at the Augsburg *Stadttheater.* He not only rejected the "classics" and their reactionary aesthetics, he ridiculed them by making them the target of a stream of overt and covert *parody.* And he went for inspiration and example to the alternative sources of a German dramatic tradition: to Baroque dramatists like Gryphius; the Austro-Bavarian folk theatre, whose last living exponent, the great beer-hall comedian Karl Valentin, became Brecht's mentor and friend; and above all to Büchner, a dramatist whose genius is today generally acknowledged to have been at least equal, if not superior, to that of Goethe or Schiller.

In Büchner's *Danton's Death* the disillusioned revolutionaries muse, before their execution, upon the futility and glory of the human condition:

We should take off our masks, and then we would see, as in a room surrounded by mirrors, everywhere but the one age-old, innumerable, indestructible dunderhead, no more, no less. The differences aren't that big, we all are rascals and angels, idiots and geniuses, all at once: these four things find room enough in the same body, they are not as voluminous as is usually assumed. To sleep, to digest, to procreate—that's what we all do; all else is mere variation on the same theme.

In Brecht's first play, *Baal,* the same note is struck by the hero, the drunken, antisocial poet Baal, and his friend the composer Ekart:

EKART. . . . . Sleep's gone to the devil and the wind again plays the organ in the willow-stumps. Thus we are left to lean against the white breasts of philosophy; the dark and the damp until the day of our blessed demise; even to the old hags no more is left than their second sight.

BAAL. In this wind you need no gin, and you are still drunk. I see the world in a mild light: it is God's excrement.

EKART. God's who has sufficiently revealed his true character once and for all by combining the genital organ with the urinary tract.

BAAL. It is all *so* beautiful.

Büchner was not yet twenty-four years old when he died in February, 1837; Brecht wrote *Baal* in 1918 when he was just twenty. Like Büchner's Danton, Brecht's Baal is a sensualist, who drifts through life, letting himself be carried by its currents, whirlpools, and eddies. There is an element of parody in Brecht's character, however: he wrote the play as an answer to a dramatized biography of the drunken playwright Grabbe by Hanns Johst, a minor expressionist who later became one of the leading Nazi poets. So Baal can *also* be seen as a *caricature* of the ridiculous worship of the overflowing vitality of genius in a certain type of German nationalist literature (which later became the worship of Hitler's "genius"). And yet, the lyrical passages Brecht gives to his antisocial giant of vitality have such force and beauty that we cannot but feel that there is a great deal of Brecht's own attitude in them. Thus Brecht's very first completed play already contains that characteristic tension that will dominate his entire *œuvre*: the tension between a desire to drift in the glorious, passive stream of life, on the one hand, and, on the other, a yearning for rationality which rejects that oceanic feeling with its passivity and amoral yielding to sensual impulse.

[16]

In the first, anarchic phase of Brecht's career, it is the sensuous, emotional, uncontrolled, passive attitude, the yielding to impulse, which dominates, while the rational, disciplined, activist attitude merely appears in the undertone of satire, mockery, ridicule with which the impulsive demeanor of the main character is portrayed. Kragler, the anti-hero of *Drums in the Night* (1919), refuses to join the Spartakist rising because he has become totally disillusioned with fighting of *any kind*, having risked his hide in the war. He decides to take his bride, who is pregnant by another man, in spite of her blemish.

Irrational selfishness is driven to its utmost limit in Brecht's most enigmatic play, *In the Jungle of the Cities* (1921–24). Two men are locked in a totally unmotivated fight to the death in a mythical Chicago largely derived from Upton Sinclair: Shlink, a middle-aged Malayan timber trader, and young Garga, whose family has come into the big city from the "Savannahs." They do not know why they are fighting; only at the end do they realize that their struggle was a desperate attempt to establish contact, human communication. "The infinite isolation of man makes enmity an unattainable goal," says Shlink. "Love, warmth from the contact of bodies, is our only mercy in the darkness. But the conjunction of bodies is the only possible one, it cannot bridge the division of language. . . . . Yes, so great is our isolation that there cannot even be a struggle." Here then, in the blind working out of irrational impulse, society itself appears as a place of icy desolation. When Shlink is dead, Garga, left alone, decides to go on living, in society. His last words—and those of the play—are: "The chaos has been used up. It was the best time."

Emotion/Reason—Selfishness/Discipline—Chaos/Order, these three polarities sum up the dialectic of Brecht's life and work. In *A Man's a Man* (1924–26) the emphasis has shifted away

from passivity: a mild little workman, Galy Gay, is here trans-
formed into a highly disciplined and ferocious soldier; from a
self-contained individualist who wallowed in chaos he is turned
into a paragon of order, a cog in a vast collective entity—a
mythical, Kiplingesque British-Indian army. In *A Man's a Man*
this process is shown satirically, as a grotesque and monstrous
act. But in *The Measures Taken* (1930) almost the same process,
the acceptance of iron, soldierly discipline by an emotional
individualist, has become a heroic act of self-abnegation cast in
the great tragic mold. For here it is not the discipline of an imperialist army, but that of the Communist party itself, which is
accepted. *Das grosse Einverständnis*—the great act of consent—
has been made the *leitmotiv* of Brecht's thinking.

The change from the anarchic to the didactic phase of
Brecht's development is clearly marked in the evolution of his
language. The Büchneresque exuberance of daring metaphors
strung together in chains of image-laden main clauses yields
to laconic severity and sparseness of expression:

> One man has two eyes
> The Party has a thousand eyes.
> The Party sees seven nations.
> One man sees one city.
> One man has his hour
> But the Party has many hours.
> One man can be destroyed
> But the Party cannot be destroyed.
> "Praise of the Party" from *The Measures Taken*

The antimilitarist and dedicated pacifist Brecht does not seem
to have noticed that he was in fact expressing the philosophy of
the Samurai, of the Prussian officer, in these stark lines, the
harsh creed of soldiers who do and die without asking the reason why. The school opera *Der Jasager* (The Yes-Sayer, 1929–
30), which also deals with the concept of the great act of

consent, is, indeed, derived from a Japanese No play (which Brecht had come to know in Arthur Waley's translation). Here a young boy whose illness impedes the progress of a party of travelers crossing a dangerous mountain range asks to be killed in the general interest. When it was pointed out to Brecht that the moral of this self-sacrificing action was questionable, he rewrote the piece with a different ending: with the boy refusing to die and declining to abide by old, inhuman customs. This new play, *Der Neinsager* (The No-Sayer), was to be performed together with the first play, which it does not replace, but complements, as an example of a *dialectical tension between two attitudes.*

In the great plays of his years of exile Brecht's style has lost the austerity of his didactic phase; and his characters, who had been reduced to the bare essentials (reminiscent of the highly stylized characters of French classical tragedy, who also lack all individual little human touches), again acquired a rich texture of personal idiosyncrasies. Nevertheless, these plays remain *didactic* in the sense that they are conceived as *parables*, models of human situations, cited, like the parables in the New Testament, not for their own intrinsic interest, but because of their general applicability to *other* human situations and problems. Galilei stands for all scientists who have submitted to the dictates of political authority (and for the atomic scientists of our time in particular); Mother Courage for all little people who do not realize that, deriving their small profit from war or the preparation of war, they are themselves guilty of causing the death of their children and the destruction of their country (as the little people of Hitler's Germany did); Puntila—evil when sober, human when drunk—is an emblem and exemplar of the irreconcilability between capitalistic attitudes and genuine humanity; while Shen Te, the good woman of Setzuan, demonstrates the impossibility of goodness in a world where survival depends on commercial success. The greatest of these plays, *The Caucasian Chalk Circle*, quite openly uses the parable form; it illustrates the solution of a problem which is posed in the prologue: who has the better right to a tract of land in a socialist country—a fairly mythically drawn Soviet Union—the legal owners or those who cultivate the land to the best purpose? The ancient legend of the child claimed by its natural and its foster mother is retold with a new variant to provide the answer. Solomon's judgment elicited a loving response from the *natural* mother and showed that it is the real mother who must also be the one who wants to spare her child pain and therefore is the one who loves it truly. In Brecht's parable it is the *foster mother* who really loves the child and refuses to hurt it, while the natural mother merely wants to use her abandoned child to reestablish her legal title to some property of which her son is heir. In other words: rather than to its legal proprietors, the land should belong to those who till it to the best effect and thereby show that they *truly love* it.

Brecht's use of the parable form expresses another aspect of his revolt against the state of German culture and the German theatre in his youth: as much as he rejected the grandiloquent classicism of the followers of Goethe and Schiller (and, to a lesser extent, of the masters themselves), he also detested the naturalistic theatre which had become dominant in Germany at the turn of the century. All of Brecht's dramatic work can be seen as a refutation of naturalism, the use of the stage to reproduce photographically accurate slices of life. The only plays he wrote in a realistic convention (*Señora Carrar's Rifles, Fears and Miseries of the Third Reich*) were propagandist potboilers. *Drums in the Night*, which takes place in a real contemporary historical and political situation (the Spartakist rising in Berlin in 1919), transcends any suspicion of realism by the exuberance of its language and Brecht's insistence on a nonrealistic set: at the end the romantically ominous blood-red moon that dominates the action is brought down and revealed to have been no more than a Chinese lantern.

As an anti-illusionist in the theatre Brecht was logically driven toward the parable form: in the austere experimental situation of a *Lehrstück,* in the fairy-tale world of distant Setzuan or the Caucasus, it is possible to deal with real problems without having to put a realistic image of the world onto the stage. For naturalism, and indeed any attempt at a realistic convention, Brecht argued, had the drawback of overindividualization. If one showed *one* family of starving, unemployed workers in loving detail, how could one convince the audience that this was not just one individual, and exceptional, case and therefore without any general validity? To do social good the theatre, Brecht felt, must be able to convince its audience that its examples were *typical* and of wide applicability. Hence he never shrank from openly drawing the moral from his examples, largely by the use of songs which stand outside the action, interrupt it, and underline its general conclusions, but also by pointed epilogues (*Puntila, The Good Woman of Setzuan*), projected slogans, etc. In the dramatic parable, distanced through the remoteness of its setting in time or space, the need for realism is greatly reduced. An audience in contemporary Germany will demand convincing realism for a play set in contemporary Germany, but will accept a highly stylized Renaissance Florence, or a picture of Germany in the Thirty Years' War, or even contemporary Finland or China. It is in these settings that the familiar can be made to appear strange so that it can be critically appraised and evaluated by an uninvolved audience.

The irony was that this doctrine of a politically efficacious

[21]

left-wing theatre fell foul of the official Communist doctrine in the Soviet Union where, after 1934, *socialist realism* had become the orthodox doctrine. In the theatre this manifested itself in a rigid insistence on the Moscow Art Theatre style of meticulous naturalism as the only permissible form of "Marxist" theatre. Great directors like Meyerhold and Tairov fell victim to this doctrine. Brecht wisely avoided settling in the Soviet Union after his exile from Germany; he even acted as co-editor of the German émigré literary magazine published in Moscow, *Das Wort*, from his home in Denmark. He attempted to conduct a mild polemic against the official doctrine: pointing to examples of progressive literature like Shelley's *Masque of Anarchy* or Swift's *Gulliver's Travels*, he argued that, after all, it was the political intention that mattered, not the form. But the essay on "The Range and Variety of the Realistic Style," which he wrote in 1938 for publication in *Das Wort*, did not see the light of day until almost twenty years later. Cautious as always, Brecht had thought better of publishing it and thus incurring the open wrath of the Stalinists.

Brecht, brought up on the grandiloquent cardboard heroism of the bombastic nationalist ideology of the Wilhelminian Reich, detested all manifestations of heroism: as Mother Courage points out, only a bad general needs brave soldiers. Mother Courage is of the same tribe as that great archetype of unheroic irony and subservient resistance, the Good Soldier Schweik as depicted in Jaroslav Hašek's immortal picaresque novel. Brecht knew and loved the book: in 1928 he had collaborated on a stage adaptation for Piscator in Berlin and during World War II he wrote a sequel to Hašek's story, the play *Schweik in the Second World War*. But there are Schweikian characters in many of his plays and prose writings; indeed, they are among Brecht's most personal creations. The character of Mr. Keuner in *The Stories about Mr. Keuner,* who quite clearly embodies Brecht's own model of himself, the man he wanted to be, is also a close relative of Schweik. The "stories" are mostly very short, ranging from one or two sentences to about a page and a half. And they attempt to portray an attitude of mind to life, or as Brecht himself said in a note preceding the first published batch of Keuner stories, "they constitute an experiment in making gestures quotable." The quotability of gestures is a key concept in Brecht's aesthetics: for Brecht the essence of art, of poetry, is, indeed, the fact that through its perfection of form, through its concentration of thought, poetry enables truth to become transmittable, accessible to the mass of people. But a merely *verbal* quotation merely transmits an abstract version of the truth. The importance of drama lies, precisely, in its concreteness, in its ability to embody actual models of *human behavior.* Instead of merely hearing people quote the noble words from some play by Shakespeare or Schiller, Brecht wanted them to repeat wholesome, rational, and noble *actions* they might have seen on the stage. Hence his desire to create *quotable gestures,* in his narrative prose as well as in his plays.

Each Keuner story embodies one *gestus.* This term, which plays an important part in Brecht's theory and practice of play-writing and play production, is not quite the same as a mere gesture. It denotes a basic human behavior model, an archetypal attitude: "A man who had not seen Mr. K. for a long time greeted him with the words: 'You have not changed at all.' 'Oh!' said Mr. K. and went pale." This Keuner story—quoted here in its entirety—does not embody a gesture (going pale could hardly be called that) but it does demonstrate a *gestus*— namely, Brecht's basic attitude that man, a rational, dialectical creature, must fear nothing more than lack of change. The more elegantly, the more thoroughly such human behavior models could be encapsuled in words and stage performance, the more readily quotable, useful, and practical they would become as tools of learning for mankind.

One of the fundamental structural principles of Brecht's epic theatre derives from the concept: each scene, Brecht postulated, should embody just one *Grundgestus* (basic *gestus*), no more and no less, and should be constructed in such a way that that basic *gestus* can be seen most clearly and to best advantage—in other words: most quotably. "The only thing Mr. Keuner had to say about style is: 'it must be quotable.' A quotation is impersonal. Who are the best sons? Those who make you forget their father." The insistence on quotability is thus a deeply anti-individualistic, antiromantic attitude. According to Brecht it is not originality which is the hallmark of the best art but, on the contrary, *typicality*, that is, the widest possible application and most general validity.

The writing of a play, in Brecht's view, as well as its production, would consist in evolving a sequence of scene-titles indicating the basic *gestus* of each scene (e.g., "Hamlet confronts his father's ghost" or "Three Witches foretell Macbeth's rise to the throne"), so that by simply putting these title captions together the whole story of the play (*Fabel*, i.e., "narrative essence") emerges.

As a follower of Watson's behaviorist school Brecht despised all psychologies based on introspection. If Stanislavsky and his followers in the techniques of "method acting" want to derive the gesture from the characters' *inner* life, Brecht was convinced that what comes first is the *attitude* which will trigger off the appropriate subjective feelings.

These views have important consequences not only for the production techniques of drama but also for the *writing* of Brecht's plays, stories, and poems. Truly dramatic language is, in the last analysis, to be considered not merely in its aspect as a structure of words, form and content but as an *action*. This is the difference between ordinary and genuinely dramatic writing. Of each sentence spoken in a play it must be possible to say *what function* it performs *as an action*. For Brecht, therefore, the problem of dramatic writing came down to the development of linguistic forms which already contain the action that inevitably must accompany them. When Othello in his final speech refers to the Turk he once met in Aleppo in order to divert the attention of the bystanders from his intention to kill himself, the words "and smote him thus" *cannot be spoken* without the sudden suicidal stab toward which they are aimed. This, to Brecht, was ideally *gestural* language, words which already contain, and which compellingly impose, the *gestus*, the attitude they embody. In this Brecht was immensely successful: the gestural quality lies in the variation of pace of the writing—the alternation of quick short words and long polysyllabic ones—in the clever use of pause and caesura, which often causes the word after the caesura to come as a shock, a surprise, and many subtle devices of rhythm, contrast, and tonal color. These are the subtleties most difficult to transfer into other languages, provided the translator is even aware of them (and that often does not seem to have been the case). Basically, a text by Brecht acts itself.

Quotability of attitude is also the principal factor in Brecht's stress on the use of songs in his plays. Here the music reinforces the gestural character of the language; for the use of music doubles the possibilities for strict control of rhythm, pace, repetition of vital phrases (refrains), and the like. And music, with the added factor of melody, increases the quotability both of the *words* (a hit tune often cannot be got out of one's consciousness, even if one wanted to get rid of it) and of the *gestus*, the attitude embodied in it.

The actor whom Brecht admired more than any other of his

[25]

time, Charlie Chaplin, also exemplifies what Brecht meant by quotable *gestus* and gestural acting. So quotable was Chaplin's characteristic grotesque walk, the way he flicked his cane, that, in his heyday, there was a Chaplin imitator (Brecht would have said a Chaplin *quoter*) at every party in the land. And these gestures which were so immensely quotable also, in a truly Brechtian sense, embodied an attitude to life: the indomitable little man's defiance of the inhuman pressures of an over-mechanized industrial society. One might formulate it in this way: as a great poet Brecht wanted to use his utmost mastery of language to force the actors appearing in his plays to act in the style of, and as brilliantly as, Chaplin.

Brecht's theory of drama, as well as his theory and practice of poetic, gestural language, ultimately amounts to a striving for simplicity, directness of structure and expression. The concentration on the clear story line (*Fabel*) in the plays and the insistence on language becoming an embodiment of simple human attitudes tend in this direction. THE TRUTH IS CONCRETE was the slogan Brecht put up over his desk wherever he came to a halt in his travels of exile.

This pursuit of directness and concreteness also can be seen as a reaction against a German tradition. Much of German poetry—and therefore also of the poetic language of drama—revels in grand philosophical abstractions and flowery, nebulous concepts. Brecht not only rejected these bombastic abstractions, he also set himself against the subjectivity, the sentimental self-involvement, of the lyrical tradition. As early as 1927 Brecht rejected any purely lyrical poetry with the argument that such poems "are simply too far removed from the original *gesture* [my italics] of the communication of a thought or emotion which would also be of use to strangers." In his first published collection of poems, *Hauspostille* (Domestic Breviary or—in

[26]

Eric Bentley's version—Manual of Piety), the poems are prefaced by "Directions for Use" which open with the words: "This Domestic Breviary is destined for the use of readers. It must not be senselessly gulped down." Clothing his scandalously free poetry in the outward guise of a prayer book was, for Brecht, an act of blasphemous irony, yet, at the same time, the analogy was also meant very seriously: a book of hymns or prayers is, after all, a genuine article of daily use, an instrument of mental and spiritual hygiene which has its clearly defined part to play in the life of pious folk. And this comes very close to Brecht's idea about the function of literature—and drama—in his ideal society.

Brecht's *Hauspostille* is typical of his first exuberant, anarchic phase. The ballads it contains celebrate a kind of wild acceptance of nature and its processes of growth and decay. The great rivers that carry the corpses of the drowned down to the sea, the jungle which engulfs the conquistadors in the wilds of Central America, the pirates who roam the seas knowing full well that one day they will be swallowed up—these are typical, ever recurring images of Brecht's early poetry. There is no introspection in these poems; even the few which deal with Brecht's personal life treat of him objectively, in the third person almost; there are no elaborate similes: the images are put before the reader directly, starkly, and stand by and for themselves. Formally there is still a good deal of artifice and elaboration: ballad metres, even sonnets, abound. The Bible, Rimbaud, Kipling (who may have been an imperialist but was also a pioneer in the use of vernacular speech, even broad dialect in poetry), and Wedekind—in his bitter, satirical cabaret songs— were the chief models of Brecht's early poetry; Goethe, Schiller, and the masters of the German Protestant hymn the chief targets for his parody.

[27]

Brecht's later poetry is more cerebral, severe, and economical. Arthur Waley's translations from the Chinese became a decisive influence: rhyme and regular rhythms were sloughed off, free verse in irregular rhythms became the norm, although for special purposes Brecht still could occasionally fall back on classical metres: he was a great believer in the hexameter as a vehicle for didactic poetry. Modeling himself on Vergil's *Georgics* and Lucretius' *De Rerum Natura,* he undertook, during his Hollywood exile, the gigantic task of putting the essence of Marxism into a great didactic poem in hexameters. He never finished the attempt, yet the remaining fragments are impressively powerful. But Brecht's best late poems are short, almost epigrammatic: they speak of the tribulations of exile, the sorrows of the poet's return to his ravaged homeland, aging, and death. They are among the finest poems in the German language. They reveal the real Brecht behind the façade of cheerful support for the East German regime; a wistful, disillusioned man, dreaming of the landscape of his childhood in Augsburg, praising the humble pleasures of homely food, cheese, bread, and cool beer. There even creeps into this private, late poetry a note of wry rejection of the hollow claims of the totalitarian state to which he had committed his fortunes. After the rising of June 17, 1953, when the regime reproached the people for their rebellion Brecht, in one famous poem, simply asked why, in that case, the government did not dissolve the people and elect itself another.

At the height of his commitment to Marxism Brecht's view of the function and nature of poetry was a severely committed one: "Lyrical poetry is never mere expression. . . . The making of poetry must be regarded as a human activity, as a social practice, with all its self-contradiction, changeability, must be seen as historically conditioned and history-making. The distinction lies between 'reflecting nature' and 'holding the mirror up' to it" (1940). On another, much earlier occasion—in 1927—Brecht had given a slightly wider definition of the function of poetry: "All great poems have the value of documents. They contain the manner of speaking of their author, an important human being." In other words: poetry is the memorable utterance of a memorable man.

Poetry thus holds a central position in any consideration of Brecht as a dramatist as well as a prose-writer. "The poet Kin [i.e., Brecht] recognized language as a tool of action." The quotation comes from another collection of pithy short aphorisms, stories, and anecdotes. *Me-Ti, the Book of Twists and Turns*, in which Brecht continued the method he adopted in the Keuner stories with the further alienation effect of a Chinese classical garb. In another passage the poet Kin (i.e., Keuner/Brecht) confesses: "How am I to write immortal works, when I am not famous? How am I to give answers, when I am not asked? Why should I lose time over writing poems, if time loses them? I write my suggestions in an enduring language, because I fear it will take a long time until they are carried out." It is to make his suggestions for social change memorable, durable enough to remain long in currency, that Brecht had to turn to poetry. It is through the power of his language to evoke the moods of action that he becomes a great playwright; through the quality of his language as a tool for the expression of thought that he becomes a great prose writer.

In his days as a struggling young playwright—that is, until his breakthrough into financial success with the *Threepenny Opera* in 1928—Brecht wrote numerous short stories for magazines, with the avowed aim of producing a readily salable product. He even won a short story competition run by one of Berlin's most popular illustrated papers. Nevertheless a good

[29]

many of these stories are little masterpieces of observation, irony, and, above all, style.

Some of these stories contain the germs of ideas which later blossomed into plays, some cast light on Brecht's psychology and the imagery of his mind: as in his early plays Brecht loved to situate his action in an Anglo-American world, somewhere between a Kiplingesque India, the "savannahs" of the American West, Jack London's arctic Alaska, Upton Sinclair's Chicago of the stockyards, and a Dickensian London teeming with quaint and sinister characters. For a young German brought up in a small town of Central Europe, but avidly reading stories of adventure, this indeed was the exotic world of romance, the wide-open spaces which beckoned those who had the courage to escape from the stuffy drawing rooms of the respectable German petty bourgeoisie.

It is in the plays *A Man's a Man* (set in Anglo-India on the borders of China and Tibet), *Threepenny Opera* (a Dickensian Victorian London with some Americanisms—the police chief is called the Sheriff), and *Mahagonny* (the brothel camp for the gold miners returning from Alaska) that the world sketched out in the short stories came to its first full fruition. Out of the *Threepenny Opera* grew Brecht's most ambitious novel, *The Threepenny Novel* (1934), a vast panorama of a pseudo-Dickensian London, brilliantly written, but marred by the extremely naïve idea of capitalism which forms the basis of its argument.

A second novel, *The Business Deals of Mr. Julius Caesar* (written 1938–39 in Denmark), remained unfinished. Here too Brecht attempted to show the sordid business reality behind the façade of glory of a great military hero and dictator, as an indictment of Hitler, whom he regarded, wrongly, as no more than the puppet of rich industrialists and businessmen. Here too there is much fine writing, but Brecht's decision to abandon it shows that he himself did not regard the work as a success.

[30]

Another somewhat fragmentary work, the series of dialogues entitled *Refugee Conversations* (largely written 1940–41 in Finland), must be counted, however, among Brecht's masterpieces. Two men stranded in Finland, Ziffel, an intellectual (who bears many features of Brecht himself), and Kalle, a worker, try to while away the time which hangs heavily on their hands by discussing the world, the war, exile, and all the countries through which they have passed. All the bitterness of exile is in these sardonic, Schweikian dialogues: "The passport is a man's noblest part. Nor does it come into being as easily as a human being. A human being can come into being in the most thoughtless manner and without good reason, but a passport—never. That is why a passport is recognized when it is a good one, while a man can be as good as he pleases and will yet not find recognition. One can say that man is no more than a stand on which to place a passport." The *Refugee Conversations* is probably Brecht's most openly autobiographical work, even more so than the Keuner stories, in which he deals with an ideal image rather than with a realistic assessment of his personality.

After his return from America to Europe Brecht compiled a slim volume of stories and narrative poems which he published in 1949 under the title *Kalendergeschichten* (Calendar Tales). Clearly designed as reading matter for the common people— German peasants in rural areas in Brecht's youth probably never read anything but the moral tales inserted between the calendar pages in their almanacs—this slim volume contains some of Brecht's finest narrative prose. The eight longer stories are in the mainstream of the tradition of the German *Novelle:* they relate significant incidents from history in a sparse, objective language, eschewing all introspection or attempts at psychological subtlety, but concentrating on the actual events. Yet these stories *give* deep psychological insights and somehow succeed in making history come alive. In "The Heretic's Coat," for example, we see the tragedy of Giordano Bruno, the natural philosopher burnt at the stake as a heretic, through the eyes of a poor tailor who had made him a coat just before he was arrested and tries to get his money for it, while the philosopher is tried and convicted.

Another story, in a quite different vein, tells of an old woman, the narrator's (and clearly Brecht's) grandmother, who, when widowed at an advanced age, shocked her village by throwing all the conventions of petty bourgeois respectability to the winds. "Thus she might rise in summer at three in the morning and take walks in the deserted streets of the little town, which she had entirely for herself. And, it was alleged, when the priest called on her to keep the old woman company in her loneliness, she invited him to the cinema."

After two years of the joys of freedom, the old woman dies: "I have seen a photograph of her which was taken for the children and shows her laid out. What you see is a tiny little face, and a thin-lipped, wide mouth. Much that is small, but no smallness. She has savoured to the full the long years of servitude and the short years of freedom and consumed the bread of life to the last crumb."

Only the terse stories of Heinrich von Kleist—another great German dramatist—can rival the economy and power of these short narratives and their mastery of German prose style.

Another large-scale project for a major novel also remained a fragment and has only recently been published: it is the so-called *Tui-Novel*, a satire, also set in a mythical China, on the corruption of the intellectuals (*Tellekt-Uell-Ins* abbreviated into *Tuis*) in the Weimar Republic. The Tuis are people who live by selling opinions. Brecht devoted a great deal of thought to this project in the thirties; it later led to the far more successful collection of brief anecdotes and sketches, *Me-Ti*, and

[32]

was finally remodeled, after Brecht's return to East Berlin in the late forties, into the material for his last play, *Turandot or the Congress of Whitewashers*. As in the case of *The Three-penny Novel* the partial failure of the Tui-project is due to Brecht's difficulty in finding a valid satirical analogy for the vices of capitalist society. That intellectuals sell their opinions is true enough, but after half a century of Communist rule in Russia, it is difficult to maintain, as Brecht certainly wanted to, that this phenomenon is the direct result of a capitalist organization of society.

Apart from his fiction Brecht left a vast and impressive corpus of other prose writings: his political articles and essays, his theoretical writings on the theatre, and—as yet unpublished, and indeed unpublishable under present circumstances in East Germany—an enormous body of diaries and letters.

Brecht's endeavors to create a truly Marxist aesthetic of theatre are brilliant and stimulating and have given rise to endless misunderstandings. Above all, it must be kept in mind that these writings do not present a unitary, finished theory but are, themselves, the documentation of a constant process of changing and developing thought. It is very significant that many of the actual practices of Brecht's playwriting and direction antedate his commitment to Marxism, so that the Marxist terminology of later writings can be seen as an attempt to find a theoretical backing for intuitions and tastes which are part of Brecht's very personal artistic approach. The same is true of much in Brecht's later theorizing: it can frequently be regarded as an ex post facto rationalization of stage inventions which emerged in rehearsal.

Indeed, in the theatre Brecht was the most empirical and undoctrinaire of directors. He conducted rehearsals at the Berliner Ensemble in the most leisurely of fashions, and entirely on a trial and error basis: every actor was given the opportunity to try out as many ways of playing a scene as he could suggest; and in the end the most effective version was chosen, after ample discussion.

The most valuable part of Brecht's theoretical work therefore appears to be that part of it which is the most concrete: the actual descriptions he gives of the way in which his plays were acted or ought to be directed. Much of this material is contained in the *model books* (for *Galileo, Mother Courage, Antigone, Señora Carrar's Rifles*) and in the copious notes which Brecht provided for editions of his plays.

Brecht's most ambitious theoretical—and practical—discussion of the theatre is contained in the voluminous fragment entitled *Der Messingkauf* (The Purchase of Brass) which Brecht began to write in 1939 and to which he added material for the rest of his life. It was to take the form of a series of dialogues interspersed with didactic poems. The title refers to the desire of one of the participants in the dialogues (The Philosopher) to find out about the true nature of theatre, and above all its usefulness for the purpose to which he wants to put it: "I feel the special nature of my interest so strongly that I see myself like a trader in brass who comes to a brass band to buy not a trumpet but merely brass." In other words: he puts the question whether the theatre, in spite of its traditional shape, could ever become the raw material for a new art, "an instrument for the imitation of certain events among people to certain purposes." The four dialogues, involving, apart from the philosopher, an actor, an actress, a *dramaturg* (literary adviser to a theatre), and an electrician, are highly stimulating and amusing; yet it is the poems, which distill the practical side of Brecht's ideas into memorable gnomic language, which prove to be the most valuable part of the unfinished edifice.

The little *Organon for the Theatre,* a compression of the theory of epic drama into seventy-seven terse paragraphs, written in 1948, is far more dogmatic and apodictic than *The Purchase of Brass:* it has given rise to far more misunderstandings.

That Brecht evolved a body of extremely fertile ideas for the writing and staging of his type of drama is beyond doubt. What is far more questionable is the basic conception that Marxism, as a philosophy, simply must produce its own, Marxist, aesthetics. Having been brought up in a German philosophical tradition, according to which each philosopher had to produce a unitary system of thought which would provide a complete world view comprising an epistemology, cosmology, logic, ethics, and aesthetics, Brecht thought that Marxism also should be able to provide all the answers to all the problems of the universe. Yet Marxism, in claiming to be a scientific system, also necessarily must be an *open* system, relying on a constant testing of its findings by experiment; moreover, basically, Marxism is a system of political economy: nobody ever attempted to construct aesthetics to fit Adam Smith's or John Maynard Keynes's ideas of political economy. Why, then, should it be necessary to complement Marxism with such a body of doctrine? Only at the point where Marxism ceases to be a scientific hypothesis and is turned into the pseudo-religion of a totalitarian state does it in fact acquire the need to have an aesthetic doctrine. As it happened, the "aesthetics" developed by Stalinism in the Soviet Union were diametrically opposed to Brecht's ideas about art and drama and corresponded, in fact, very closely to those of Hitler's Germany (rejection of all abstract and experimental art as degenerate). In other words: the aesthetics actually developed by Soviet Communism were not Marxist but *totalitarian* aesthetics, and derived not from any

[35]

philosophy but from the needs of thought-control in a dictatorship. Indeed, Brecht's insistence that the theatre should shock its audience into critical thought made his aesthetics highly suspect in the eyes of the Stalinists and their successors.

There remains the problem about the philosophical implications of the theory of genres enunciated by Goethe and Schiller: that drama, by its insistence that what the audience sees is something which happens here and now and with which they can totally identify, presupposes that human nature is constant and unchangeable. It was this which led Brecht to reject the idea of a *dramatic* theatre altogether, and to opt for an *epic* theatre. Yet the implications of the "Aristotelian" conception of drama as understood by Goethe and Schiller need not be quite so drastic. The declared purpose of this conception of drama *might* be that, human nature being always the same, the spectators ought to be made to identify themselves with the actions of the characters on the stage. Yet, as social conditions change, in fact, the vast bulk of past drama fails to bring about any identification, becomes, indeed, unperformable. Most of the emotions portrayed in eighteenth-century larmoyant comedy, in Victorian melodrama, are incapable of arousing any echo in the minds of contemporary audiences, except perhaps ribald laughter. Only a very small proportion of the drama of past epochs still has the power of making contemporary spectators identify with the experience of characters like Oedipus, Lear, Juliet, or Othello. Yet, it could be argued, it is not with the slave-owning ancient king that audiences identify while watching Oedipus but with the man who feels guilty for having desired his own mother; not with the Moorish general but with the jealous husband; not with the Veronese aristocratic girl but with a girl kept from marrying the man she loves; not with the mythical ruler of a barbaric Britain but with an old man ousted

[36]

by his daughters. In these cases the social framework behind the characters may have changed decisively, yet in their basic emotional aspects there has been little or no change. In his effort to make his actors see such characters critically Brecht wrote "practice scenes" to be performed during rehearsals. One of these shows Romeo and Juliet being extremely heartless in their relations to their servants, to whom they deny the freedom of having high-flown emotions like their own love. Thus Brecht wanted his actors—and the audience—to be made aware that in feudal Verona only the masters could indulge in romantic love. That is a valid point, but not the point that Shakespeare wanted to make; why then should Shakespeare's play be used to yield this message rather than the one about young love which *is* still valid? Likewise, husbands still tend to be as jealous as Othello. Yet, Brecht argued, they should not be made to feel that they agree with Othello; by inhibiting their tendency to identify with him, the husbands in the audience should be made to see how foolish such jealousy, based as it is on a medieval concept of ownership, must be. Yet the strong tendency toward identification in contemporary audiences exists precisely because these medieval concepts still hold sway, in spite of totally different social conditions. Once a more enlightened age has dawned, when the emancipation of women is complete and love is freed from any ownership concepts, *Othello* will automatically carry its "alienation effect," without any effort on the part of directors or theoreticians.

Conversely, in Brecht's own plays the alienation effect invariably fails in performance whenever the emotions portrayed are of such a nature that they correspond to those of the audience: Brecht wanted the audience to criticize Mother Courage for her involvement with war as a business, to condemn her for causing the death of her children. But in spite of songs, anti-illusionist staging, posters with the exact time and date, the distancing effect does not take place; the mothers in the audience—and not only they—still identify with the predicament of a loving mother who loses her children. Brecht scolded critics and audiences alike for seeing Mother Courage as a Niobe. But they did, and thereby showed clearly that the world of Oedipus and the other archetypes of Greek myth retains its power, that not only might modern audiences identify with Oedipus, but that the even most consciously Marxist conception of a character could ultimately not escape identification with a human type dating back to antiquity. And what is true of Mother Courage also applies to Puntila (whom audiences find lovable because they cannot but identify with his drunkenness); to Galilei (whose sensuousness and cowardice produce similar effects of sympathetic empathy); to Azdak and many other "alienated" characters.

This is not to say that Brecht's *technique* of alienation does not produce results of supreme artistic quality. Precisely *because* the human tendency toward identification is so strong, the continued efforts to inhibit it produce a tension, a tug-of-war between opposing tendencies which, ultimately, creates a kind of double vision, an equal stimulation of intellect and emotion, and an effect of depth, of a multitude of levels of meaning.

Hence—and this is a characteristically Brechtian paradox—those of his works which are most openly political, and therefore unidimensional, invariably turn out to be the weakest.

When a play lacks human, or indeed political, *truth*, it invariably fails to produce identification among the spectators: they notice the author's intention and resent being manipulated.

Brecht's case is a most illuminating illustration of the problems of politically committed art. Where a ready-made political concept is dominant in his mind, even a writer of genius like Brecht cannot make it the basis of a wholly convincing work of art. The political stereotype inhibits the free play of the artist's imagination and forces him to create oversimplified characters and situations. Where, on the other hand, the political motivation is an indirect one, where it springs from the poet's *experience* of the injustice and suffering caused by the state of the world, and where therefore he is able to give his imagination free rein, so that the characters can develop in the three-dimensional roundness of natural growth, the result is not only a greater human impact but also, ultimately, a greater social and *political* effectiveness even though that political effect may not always be the one which had been in the poet's mind.

The history of Brecht's impact on the world and the spread of his fame clearly illustrates the validity of this analysis. In vain do the followers of the totalitarian party line accuse those who make this point of trying to turn Brecht into a harmless article of aesthetic consumption and denying him his own claim to be more, namely a revolutionary force that effectively will and can change society itself. Yet the fact remains that Brecht is as frequently and successfully performed in the Western world as in East Germany and that, indeed, his message of critical detachment has a more explosive effect in the East, where it appears antitotalitarian, than in the West, where it can easily be taken for granted. The *Threepenny Opera* ran in New York for many years, yet it will be hard to find anyone who was converted by it to a Marxist view of politics.

That this is so makes Brecht a failure only in the eyes of those who measure the values of aesthetics according to political standards. Nobody wants to deny the enormous benefits Brecht derived artistically from his commitment to Marxism: but these benefits were of a personal nature and affected his work as a

[39]

poet and playwright only indirectly. Of course a dramatist derives great advantages from having a firm philosophy of life, a clear allegiance and purpose. If one considers the wild exuberance of Brecht's early work and its undertone of despair, one realizes how dangerous it would have been for him, as an artist and as a human being, if he had failed to find such a firm allegiance. The short-term political objectives of any work of art, however, are bound to be the ones most subject to being overtaken by events, to becoming obsolete and even incomprehensible. Who, today, pays any attention to the fact that a play like Shakespeare's *Richard II* was brimful of political implications to an audience who had lived through the Essex rebellion? That does not diminish the human and aesthetic values contained in the play. In the long view, therefore, the only thing which remains relevant in a work of art is its artistic value. A seventeenth-century musket may have become obsolete as a weapon, while it still remains beautiful as a work of craftsmanship. Brecht's plays might have been fashioned by him as weapons, but their aesthetic values will remain valid long after the conflicts to which they were relevant have been forgotten.

What does matter in a major artist, apart from his talent, however, is the depth and quality of his human experience: Brecht is unique among the great artists of his time in that—by the fact of his commitment—he was more deeply involved in the experience of his epoch than almost any other poet of comparative stature. He was directly affected by World War I as well as World War II; he had firsthand experience of what will probably be the archetypal predicament of the twentieth century: political exile; he experienced vicious persecution by the Nazis, was deeply involved with the Soviet Union, lived in the United States and became a victim of the anti-Communist witchhunt of the forties; and at the end of his life, in Communist East Berlin, he took a stand against totalitarian Stalinism which foreshadows the renewal of Marxist thought in the Poland of the fifties and the Czechoslovakia of the late sixties. He was equally at home in the turbulent Berlin of the dying Weimar Republic, in the Moscow of the Stalinist purges, and in the torrid climate of postwar Hollywood and New York. He saw Soviet friends, like Tretyakov, hounded to their deaths by Stalin, and Hollywood friends, like Chaplin, persecuted as subversive elements in America. He witnessed the rise and fall of Hitler, had his books burned by the Nazis, and fifteen years later stood on the ruins of Hitler's Reichskanzlei.

It is this experience which shines through Brecht's poetry and the best of his prose work and dramatic output: what is remarkable is that his reaction, though frequently violent and impatient, basically amounts to a grim determination to survive and to transcend all the brutality and fanaticism by an ideal of *friendliness*. This is a concept that owes much to a classical Chinese Confucian view of an ideal society based on mutual politeness and respect. Brecht's poetry in the last years of his life was deeply imbued with these almost quietist, Stoic values, which combine the attitudes of the Good Soldier Schweik and the serenity of Horace with the Confucian ideal.

All this is a far cry from the wild rebellion of Brecht's youth and yet is strangely consistent with the dialectics of his development from a feeling of emotional passivity and helplessness in the face of the uncontrollable, cataclysmic forces of history, society, and man's own instincts, to a yearning for discipline, rationality, and conscious control over nature and man through science, to an ultimate synthesis of a humble recognition of man's ability to master his environment, tempered by a resolve to do his best within his modest capacity.

Brecht's *œuvre*, therefore, must always be judged as a whole;

the more deeply committed of his disciples have, in the past, made considerable efforts to minimize, and even to suppress, the more chaotic outpourings of the early Brecht. He himself rewrote his first play to reach the stage, *Drums in the Night*, before he included it in the collected edition of his plays in 1954. It is not widely realized how radical some of his alterations were in comparison with the rare first edition, the text of which has never been reprinted. The difficulties arising from the curious position that Brecht's collected works are being published in West Germany, while the archives containing the manuscripts are in East Berlin, have made the publication of a really authoritative and acceptable text of Brecht works almost impossible. Here lies one of the chief dangers for Brecht's posthumous reputation and true appreciation, and also one of the chief tasks for true Brecht scholarship of the future. The confusions caused by the existence of a "collected" edition which is known to omit some very important texts—such as Brecht's critical poems about Stalin—and which publishes other texts without a clear indication of how they differ from earlier versions of the same work will become progressively worse as time goes on. Nor can a state of affairs be defended which keeps the diaries and letters unpublished for the foreseeable future.

It must also be realized that the absence of a reliable text further complicates the already highly complicated situation with regard to translations: once a translation exists it tends to become the authoritative text in its own language; readers who have no German are in no position even to try to compare the text they have before them with other, earlier versions and in the course of time it will become increasingly difficult to disentangle variants caused by mistranslation or misunderstandings from those deriving from the use of differing texts as starting points for different translations.

[42]

Most unfortunate of all for the growth of genuine appreciation and a deeper understanding of Brecht's greatness as a poet is the unscrupulous and stupid use made of his fame by the official propaganda in East Germany. Not only does this lead to suppression of hitherto unpublished texts, the spreading of falsifications and legends about the circumstances of his life; it also inevitably produces a backlash on the other side. That a leading West German politician should have compared Brecht to the author of the Nazi anthem, Horst Wessel, was an act of the most glaring and tasteless stupidity. It sprang from complete ignorance of Brecht's *œuvre* and was based on no more than a reading of the equally stupid and tasteless totalitarian propaganda about Brecht's supposed stalwart support of the Ulbricht-Stalin line. Fortunately that reaction has now worn off in West Germany and other Western countries: Brecht is more frequently, more widely performed—and with a greater variety of his work—in West than in East Germany or indeed Eastern Europe. What is most unfortunate, however, is that the championing of Brecht by the Ulbricht Stalinists has led to his rejection by the New Left, the students in West Germany and, indeed, in many East European countries. They have come to regard Brecht as an "establishment author" of the Stalinist "new class." This is the bitterest cut of all, the one which Brecht himself would have feared most, and the least justified. It is ironical that the young generation of freethinking Communists in Czechoslovakia, for example, should have written off Brecht on this score. For history will finally show that he was one of the earliest pioneers of their very thinking.

That, ultimately, all these difficulties will be overcome seems, however, certain, simply because Brecht's stature as one of the major forces of twentieth-century literature is assured. The multitude of problems which Brecht's personality, his biog-

[43]

raphy, and the text of his works offers to scholars is, in itself, a further guarantee of his continuing fame: there is so much still to be elucidated, so many crucial points to be established, and much merit and reputation to be won in exploring Brecht's life and work.

He himself would have looked at all this activity with wry amusement. His publisher has revealed that, when the first attempt was made at issuing a collected edition of the plays, Brecht insisted on fairly large print and small format so that his output might be made to look more substantial on the bookshelves. He thus had a modest idea of his own *œuvre*, and probably did not feel that a good deal of the material posthumously published really belonged to the enduring body of his work. In the early thirties he had issued his work in progress in modest gray brochures entitled *Versuche* (Experiments) and in these he had always cited a number of names beside his own, as *Mitarbeiter* (collaborators). Brecht looked at the poet's work as a craft comparable to that of medieval architects or painters who either remained anonymous or worked collectively, with a number of disciples taking part in painting one picture. He rejected the romantic ideal of the unique original genius and ridiculed the myth of divinely inspired creativity.

And yet—with the characteristic dialectical tension between opposites within his personality—he was, at the same time, aware of his importance as an artist. When, during his American period, a friend pointed out to him that he had used an Anglicism in something he had written, and that the expression concerned did not exist in German, he retorted: "Well, then, it exists from now on."

Similarly, having ridiculed the worship accorded to the "classics" of German literature in schools and universities and among the educated classes, he himself occasionally referred to himself as a classic.

[44]

And that is what, inevitably, he has become: it is Brecht's unique achievement that he has reconciled two traditions in German literature which had been kept in different compartments before him, a state of affairs which had had most unfortunate effects on the cultural life of Germany. In Brecht the rough, plebeian, popular tradition and the sophisticated, academic, refined, respectable tradition have come together. Thanks to Brecht's achievement the work of the Austro-Bavarian folk comedians and the plays of the *poètes maudits* of the eighteenth and early nineteenth centuries appear in a new light and have assumed a new importance. And what is more: by introducing his new rough, popular, almost dialect tone, Brecht succeeded in forging a new German stage idiom, which is neither the highly refined, but unnatural *Bühnendeutsch* (stage German) of the one nor the broad vernacular regional speech of the other tradition. This is an achievement which has greatly eased the difficulties of the generation of young postwar dramatists and poets in Germany.

Moreover, with his preference for exotic foreign locations in his youth, with his experience of Scandinavia, the Soviet Union, and the United States in his years of exile, Brecht has done much to break down the provincialism of much of German dramatic literature. And at the same time, having achieved international success, Brecht has put Germany on the map of international drama once again. So Brecht, the outsider and rebel, has a solid claim to enduring fame.

Not that Brecht hankered after posthumous recognition. Indeed at times he insisted that he dreaded nothing more than elevation to the status of a classic, which to him meant condemnation to ultimate innocuousness as safe reading matter for school children. He wanted his work to become an active agent for genuine change in the social and cultural condition of man. But for the fact that *he* had lived the tyrants might have sat a little more securely on their thrones. That was his hope. It is, however, more than doubtful whether Hitler's fall was speeded even by a second through the exertions of Brecht and other anti-Nazi intellectuals. On the other hand, Brecht's support hardly strengthened the position of that other tyrant, Stalin, by as much as one whit. *Can* the exertions of writers like Brecht change the social condition of man at all? Only indirectly: by changing man's sensibility, the atmosphere, the moral climate that surrounds him. But whether Brecht's view was correct or not, his striving in its tragic irony raises the matter of the artist's importance with the impact of a major test case. And for that, as well as for the beauty and depth of his poetry, Brecht merits a place among the great writers of his time.

SELECTED BIBLIOGRAPHY

BRECHT'S WORKS IN GERMAN

Gesammelte Werke (Collected Works). 20 vols. (paperback) or 8 vols. (hardback India paper edition). Frankfurt, Suhrkamp, 1967.

PRINCIPAL WORKS AVAILABLE IN ENGLISH TRANSLATION

Seven Plays. Ed. with an introduction by Eric Bentley. New York, Grove Press, 1961.

Plays. 2 vols. London, Methuen, 1960 and 1962.

Parables for the Theatre (The Caucasian Chalk Circle and The Good Woman of Setzuan). Tr. by Eric and Maja Bentley. New York, Grove Press, n.d.

Baal; A Man's a Man; and The Elephant Calf. Ed. Eric Bentley. New York, Grove Press, 1964.

Mother Courage. Tr. Eric Bentley. New York, Grove Press, 1963.

Jungle of Cities and Other Plays. New York, Grove Press, 1966.

The Jewish Wife and Other Short Plays. New York, Grove Press, 1965.

The Visions of Simone Machard. Tr. Carl R. Mueller. New York, Grove Press, 1965.

The Threepenny Opera. Tr. Desmond Vesey, with lyrics by Eric Bentley. New York, Grove Press, 1964.

Galileo. Tr. Charles Laughton. New York, Grove Press, 1966.

Edward II. Tr. Eric Bentley. New York, Grove Press, 1966.

Manual of Piety (Hauspostille). Tr. Eric Bentley. New York, Grove Press, 1966.

Brecht on Theatre. Tr. John Willett. London, Methuen, 1964. (A collection of Brecht's theoretical writings.)

The Messingkauf Dialogues. Tr. John Willett. London, Methuen, 1965.

Tales from the Calendar. Tr. Yvonne Kapp and Michael Hamburger. London, Methuen, 1961.

The Threepenny Novel. Tr. D. L. Vesey and C. Isherwood. New York, Grove Press, 1956.

BIBLIOGRAPHIES

Nubel, Walter. Bertolt Brecht-Bibliographie, in *Sinn und Form*. Zweites Sonderheft Bertolt Brecht. East Berlin, 1957.

Petersen, Klaus Dietrich. Bertolt-Brecht-Bibliographie. Bad Homburg v.d.H., Verlag Gehlen, 1968.

BOOKS ON BRECHT

Brandt, Thomas O. Die Vieldeutigkeit Bertolt Brechts. Heidelberg, Lothar Stiehm Verlag, 1968.

Chiarini, Paolo. Bertolt Brecht. Bari, Laterza, 1959.

Demetz, Peter, ed. Brecht: A Collection of Critical Essays. Englewood Cliffs, N.J., Prentice-Hall, 1962.

Dort, Bernard. Lecture de Brecht. Paris, Seuil, 1960.

Esslin, Martin Brecht: The Man and His Work. Garden City, N.Y., Doubleday, 1960.

Ewen, Frederic. Bertolt Brecht: His Life, His Art and His Times. New York, Citadel Press, 1967.

Fassmann, Kurt. Brecht, eine Bildbiographie. Munich, Kindler, 1958.

Gray, Ronald. Brecht. Edinburgh, Oliver and Boyd, 1961.

Grimm, Reinhold. Bertolt Brecht. 2d ed. Stuttgart, Metzler, 1963.

Kesting, Marianne. Bertolt Brecht in Selbstzeugnissen und Bilddokumenten. Reinbek bei Hamburg, Rowohlt, 1959.

Mayer, Hans. Bertolt Brecht und die Tradition. Pfullingen, Neske, 1961.

Rischbieter, Henning. Bertolt Brecht. 2 vols. Velber bei Hannover, Friedrich, 1966.

Ruelicke-Weiler, Kaethe. Die Dramaturgie Brechts. East Berlin, Henschel, 1966.

Schuhmann, Klaus. Der Lyriker Bertolt Brecht, 1913–1933. East Berlin, Ruetten and Loening, 1964.

Schumacher, Ernst. Die dramatischen Versuche Bertolt Brechts, 1918–1933. East Berlin, Ruetten and Loening, 1955.

————. Drama und Geschichte—Bertolt Brechts "Leben des Galilei." East Berlin, Henschel, 1965.

Spalter, Max. Brecht's Tradition. Baltimore, Md., Johns Hopkins Press, 1967.

Willett, John. The Theatre of Bertolt Brecht. Norfolk, Conn., New Directions, 1959.